Empowered
Design

Empowered Design

A DESIGN PLAN FOR LIVING

Blanche Garcia

ISBN: 0692793887
ISBN 13: 9780692793886

Preface

My definition of Empowered Design: When Interior Design and Energy Design collide. Now most of us know what Interior Design is, but I'm sure you're wondering what in god's name is Energy Design. And no, I'm not referring to "GREEN" or "Energy Efficient Design." I refer to Energy Design as the designing of the emotional and non-physical space that surrounds you, or that affects you on a daily basis. Empowered Design is about creating the life that you are meant to live starting from the inside out. Design is all encompassing; from creating a passionate plan for life, to your personal space supporting your energy.

Let's face it, Designers are like therapists and we are the go-to people for our clients, not only for style but also for life advice. It takes hard work and determination to live your best life! Just so we get off on the right foot, I am not perfect, but I've also left no stone unturned along the way in achieving my daily version of personal success.

But why write a book now? Because I have this force that's inside of me that needs to show you what's behind the curtain. Trust me, it's a trait that my mother could do without. With every success, there were and are a million tiny steps and setbacks. We all have a story, and when we can be honest with our own, then that's when you are able to create a mirror for someone else to look through, to their own humanity. I didn't set out to write a memoir, because isn't that something you're supposed to write on your way out the door? But I wouldn't be honest if I didn't share the stories that went along with the lessons that I have learned. So, the truth is that I have fought my whole life to find out who I am, where I fit in, and to be who I am, regardless of what other people wanted me to be.

I hope that I can make you laugh along the way, and help you to understand that where you started and where you are right now, doesn't define you. You don't have to settle for halfway happy. People go their whole lives thinking that the only options they have are the ones in front of them. But you can make your own options. When you find out who you are and what you want out of your life, then the scary parts aren't so scary anymore. Because you know that you got this! And that's the kind of confidence that comes from knowledge of self.

As you will read in the chapters ahead, books have always been and will always be my greatest teacher. Reading gave me access to people that normally wouldn't give me the time of day. I always felt when I read a book, that it made me rethink things in a different way, and that I was being handed the keys to my future. I may not have been the smartest girl nor the richest, but when I walked into a bookstore, I had access to all of the treasures of the world. To this day, the smell of a bookstore gets me going quicker than a sale at Barneys. My dad would say that street smarts beats book smarts any day. While I agree, I figured that you can't be taught street smarts, but I can and should learn some book smarts. Two super powers are better than one, right? So let me show you what you can achieve when you mix street smarts and books smarts together with a heavy dose of what my dad would call moxie. Look it up, it's a real word!

Intro

ven though you live in a world with gazillions of people (and yes, I'm aware that's not technically a real word) it all comes down to YOU. You are the one experiencing it, and you are the only one to blame when the curtain comes down if you didn't like the show. I will show you ways to figure out who you are, what you want, and best of all how to get what you want. Knowing what you want to achieve out of this life is sometimes easier than figuring out how to change your mindset from living in lack to living in abundance. I was 12-years old when I realized that I didn't want to live in lack anymore and I was going to do anything in my power to change it. My father had just died and our cars were taken away, and the creditors (which he was barely keeping at bay) smelled blood. I decided then and there that I was in charge of my own destiny, and that I had a choice to make. Do I turn that moment into a lifetime of living and identifying with lack, or do I choose abundance as my life path? At the time, I didn't have the right words to explain those feelings, but I knew I had a choice on how I reacted. I find it interesting that at 12-years old, I was able to summarize something about life that to this day I find to be the ultimate truth. I could either let life happen to me or I can make my life happen. I think my journey really started at that moment; the moment when I realized my need to be something more than my circumstances.

So, as I learned, so will you. No matter from what age you start or from what walk of life that you come from, we all have the gift of deciding how we react to the situations that life throws at us, and who we ultimately want to be. Everyone has the mistaken belief that life controls you, when really you have more of a say in it than you realize. It's time to learn how to get out of your own way, tune out the white noise and start living life on purpose. How many times do people ask you how you're doing and you use the same boiler plate answer "good?" Why settle for "good" when you can start getting used to "great!" Look at it this way, just because you're not sick may mean that you're not dying, but it also means that you're not thriving either. There is a very big difference between the two. You know the scariest part of all of this is deciding something has to change. I'm not alone in feeling like you should be happy with everything you have, because there is always someone else out there who has less. But at the end of the day there's a knowing that something just doesn't feel right or doesn't fit into the puzzle. It's the same knowing that everything looks like it should on paper, but in real time...not so much.

I wanted and still want more out of life than what I'm being handed. Because what you're being handed is just a small part of what is possible. The fact that you're reading this book shows that you want more too. There is an art to knowing how to navigate this world and those who have the right map are the winners in their own life. You're not only going to have the map, you're going to have a newly-tuned compass when you're done with this book.

Because what good is a map if your intuitive compass is unbalanced. You will always be led back to the beginning.

Since designing a plan for living includes everything in it, you will address not only your mental clutter but your physical clutter as well. It's true what they say; a cluttered space equals a cluttered mind. How are you expected to breathe if you're literally surrounded by years of baggage? You will now create a clear path to a fresh beginning. With this new space, you will have room to visualize and create a passionate plan for your new future. When you close the last page of this book you will have skills that you never even knew that you possessed. You already possess all the tools that you need; you just need a little help re-organizing the design of it all.

CHAPTER 1

And YOU are?

**It's a lot easier to decide who you don't want to be
than to figure out who you are.**

t all starts with you, but have you thought about who you are? You can't decide to change your life if you have no idea how you got here in the first place. So, let's start at zero and build from there, shall we? If I'm going to share with you all the fruits of my tree, then I have to also show you some of the weeds I had to pull along the way. Cause let me tell you, we all have weeds—just some roots go deeper than others.

Let's get real basic and start with the two people that will always be the biggest influences in my life…my parents. Both are the strongest people I know, but they each have different kinds of strength that has manifested in different ways throughout my life. I think if I explain a little of where I came from you will understand the kind of stock I'm made of. It's not that I was a Kennedy or a Martian or anything like that, but my childhood was something like out of the movies, I guess you could say. I never thought my life was different than anyone else's until much later. My father was this larger-than-life teddy bear that would shower me with love, gifts and toys...and more toys. Oh, and let's not forget the jewelry. Yes, you heard right...I said jewelry. What...don't all five-year old's get diamonds?

To clarify, my father was in the "family." For those of you who aren't from New Jersey or New York, that's a nicer way of saying that my father was in the mob. He was what we called a shylock. If you actually google the definition, it runs something along the lines of a person who lends money at an extortionate rate of interest. My mother met my father at a time when she was looking for an apartment to rent. My aunt suggested that my mom go talk to my dad at one of his night clubs, because he owned some "real-estate." My dad took one look at my mom and fell in love. It was a real mafia love story complete with his wife and kids. Hey that was the lifestyle! But it was true love for him, because no matter how hard it was and unheard of at the time, my father ended up marrying my mother and we became a family. That's right; the scandalous headline in the neighborhood went something like "Mob guy divorces his Italian wife to marry his Puerto Rican mistress!" You can feel the judgment to this day.

To me it was normal that my dad had a bunch of my so-called uncles (who had names like Uncle Bunko or Uncle Bubbie) over every week for a guy's night in the dining room. I believe the proper term would be a sit-down. I did wonder why even though my dad's name was John, everyone called him Biggie. My dad told me that when he was born, that he was a big boy. My grandfather being right off the boat from Cuba had an accent. He kept saying that my dad was a big boy, but in his accent, it sounded more like "biggeee boy." So, everyone called my dad Biggie. My life included lots of loud parties with tons of family, and people that were called family regardless of the actual relation. We had houses and tons of cars, and yes, jewelry. He owned a few businesses and I'm not quite sure of all of them. There were restaurants, nightclubs, a furniture delivery company, a jewelry company, oh, and I'm pretty sure one of them was the manufacturing of work-out equipment. Bottom line: he was an entrepreneur.

My mom was like this glamorous beautiful star. My dad used to say she was the strongest broad he knew. He used words like broad because where I come from it's a compliment. She would go out and find all the bands to play in my dad's nightclub. She always took me everywhere with her, shopping for clothes, food, you name it. Mom was always dressed to the nine's and I would see men almost break their neck to turn around when she walked by. But my clearest memory of her is when she was getting ready to go out with my dad to his club. I would watch with wide-eyes as she sat at her vanity and put on her makeup and perfume, while she decided which of her many jewels from her jewelry closet that she was going to wear that night. I would try on her high heels and jewelry while she was getting dressed, all the while thinking how beautiful she was and how I couldn't wait to grow up and have my own of...well all of it!

I would later learn when my father died just how strong she was. She cleaned houses to keep a roof over our head, took in roommates so that we could stay in our house, and she showed me the true meaning of tenacity. As normal as life seemed to me as a child, I think the larger-than-life people and scenarios showed me the larger-than-life wins and losses. That everything is possible and fleeting at the same time. One day you're up and one day you're down. I learned early on that you have to fight for what you want because there are no guaranties, as cliché as that sounds. Looking back now I realize as I write this book that my father showed me that you could be anything that you want, that the labels you start out with in life don't define you. I mean he started out with a produce cart in Brooklyn so that he could help support his brothers and sisters, and he made himself into a man that could walk into any room and have people eating out of the palm of his hand. He never saw barriers between who he was and what he wanted to be, and I think that the kind of nerve that it took for him to reach for anything that he wanted taught me more about how to navigate life than any book could have.

How to connect the dots

So, I went forward into the world sure of a few things; I loved beautiful objects, I could play any role that I wanted, and that it was just as easy to fly high as it was to fall down. I think because I saw such extremes in how life could be, it never occurred to me that I couldn't be everything that I wanted to be, and all at the same time. I think it's why I hate labels to this day; it feels limiting. So, when I decided at the ripe old age of sixteen that I was going to be a designer, I didn't necessarily decide of what I would be a designer of. I just wanted to create beautiful things for people to enjoy.

In order to bring out the best in people within their spaces, you really have to understand who you are first. When I started, design was something I gave to other people, simply based on reaction. I was reacting to what other people requested of design, kind of like a filter you would say. I would see beautiful buildings, but it was just something that I would experience, but not something I connected with. I think it was around the same time that I had this epiphany, that design was just as much about what you experience as it is about how you connect to it. I felt very much pigeonholed into thinking I had to choose one form of design, it was either interior design or fashion design etc., and once you chose a path then that's where you had to stay. I think that's what happens when you listen to what other people tell you more than you listen to how you feel inside.

But as I continued on my journey of self-awareness, career and everything that goes into this mixed bag of what you call life, I started to see that design meant much more to me. The more aware you are about what you don't want; you realize that you don't have to label what you do want. I started designing my life to look much more about how I dreamed it could be. And my dreams included so many different things, some of which were opposites of each other, and some that bled into one another. I started allowing myself to see it all as one design without judging what that meant.

I was just having a conversation last night with a girlfriend of mine, and we were talking about relationships. But I feel that the same reasoning applies to life in general, as well. She was saying how hard it is to meet someone as you get older, and how easy it was when we were younger. I told her my take on it; that it's only harder because you have learned what you don't want, and by doing so, you've tightened up the list of what you do want. When you're younger, you don't necessarily use quality control. It's more about what falls into your lap or what comes easy. Figuring out who you are and what you want in life doesn't always make life easier, but you do end up a whole lot happier. At least it should!

You see, all of it is one big design, what your outside looks like, what your interior world looks like, and it's all connected. In order for me to tackle the outside world, I had to tackle who I was on the inside world. Once I realized that "it" and "we" are all connected I was able to really start playing with design and playing with how I affected people's lives within design. It's so funny that I tell my clients not to stick themselves in a box of one form of style. People like to categorize themselves as either "traditional," "modern," and when they don't know what they are they then call themselves "transitional." I would ask them, why are you thinking that you're only one tonal? Learn to see the intricate connections and designs that make up life, this will give you a starting point on where to create change.

Taking off the labels that you and other people put on yourself can be very hard to do. But in order to start with a clean slate you have to look at yourself with new eyes. Look at your life as if there were no road blocks and start to see how everything is interlaced. Think about it; when you don't like what you're wearing, it can throw your whole day off. When your house is a mess, your mind is a mess. The opposite is true as well; when you don't have your life put together, then all the beautiful clothes and houses in the world won't make it better. It is all a domino effect; you can't change one part without affecting the whole.

Exercise 1: I want you to take a pen and a piece of paper and quickly without thinking write down ten words that describe who you are. Now look at that list and see if you can cross out any words that are a description that others tell you that you are, words that you don't feel a connection to. Next to that list, in a separate column, write down as many words as you want that would describe how you would like others to see you. This is a list that describes who you could be if there were no judgements and no obligations. Put this list aside for later.

What does your map say?

You have to consciously manifest, which not only means feeling in a direction or moving in a direction, it also means landing in a direction. This is not something that is given to you at birth; nobody gives you a map of how to design the life you want. This is because the way your life looks and how you get there is unique to you as an individual. Each journey is different, so obviously how you get there will be different then the person next to you. Each turn that you make, and that you are making at this very moment, is made up of a thousand tiny invisible decisions that manifested into something that put you on one course or another. If you're really quiet, you'll see that you have your instincts to lead the way. We all have this natural compass, which is the only thing that you really need to guide you. It took me a long time to learn how to use it, and believe it or not, it's so easy to connect to. We have just taught ourselves to ignore it. Once you cue into it, it will make navigating your map much easier.

So, here's how it goes: close your eyes and think of a decision that you have to make that has been bothering you. It can be something small or large, but something that has been weighing on your mind. Let's say that you have two possible solutions to your decision. We will call them option A and option B. Keeping your eyes shut, imagine that you have chosen option A. Visualize yourself in the physical scenario that would go along with it. Now check in with your body, with the sensations that come up for you. Does your stomach tighten? Do you feel it high in your stomach or low in your stomach? Take note, and now imagine that you chose scenario B. Visualize yourself in the scenario that would accompany the second option. Now check in with yourself to see where you feel the sensation in your body. Is there a difference to how your body reacted to either option? You may have to practice this a few times to tune in to how your body communicates to you which way you should go. For me, I always feel a tingling sensation high in my stomach, when it's a decision that feels right. And I always feel the dead weight of a rock at the pit of my stomach, when it's not a direction that I should take.

You are the only one who can know if something is right for you. When all the chatter and opinions cloud your mind, turn to yourself to gage what the right thing for you is. Your life has to be authentic to who you are. It's like breathing air. If you make decisions based on what other people think are right for you, you can never take full ownership of the highs and lows. If you take a wrong turn, at least it was your wrong turn to make. When you take a wrong turn while following someone else's map then you run the risk of always playing the "what if" game. Growing up there were plenty of times that my mom and I disagreed about how I should live my life. I would always say to her that I could live with my mistakes but I could never live with the mistakes that I made based on someone else's decisions. Believe it or not, no matter how young I was at the time, I must have still recognized that I would own my decisions long after everyone else was gone. Because of this I have never blamed anyone else for my decisions, and I have always chosen to learn from my wrong turns. In the end, there are no wrong turns after all, just changes in the route.

It takes the courage of a warrior to find out who you are and even more so to then move in that direction. The easiest thing to do in this life is to follow someone else's dream or roadmap. It's so easy that that's exactly what most people do. And even making a decision on which direction to go is very hard, because that means that you have to say no to all of the other options. This is why they call it commitment. Because you have to be able to commit to a direction, and see it through, even when it seems like it's never going to work. That's where faith kicks in.

When I finished school, and started working in the real world, it occurred to me that I had bitten off more than I could chew. The more I learned about design the more I realized that I needed to learn about design. Oh, and I felt so intimidated by my peers in the field. They went to better schools and had better jobs, and they were so creative! I couldn't even remember anything I had learned in school, let alone get a job or a client. I mean a paying client, not your girlfriend whose room you did for free and who says you did a great job, as the paint is literally crying down her walls. You see, I failed to do the most important step, I failed to plan. Now I can't be too hard on myself because I didn't know anyone in my field, and I had no guidance or mentor to show me how it's done.

I just assumed that you went to school and rested on your talent, and when you graduated that you would be handed the career of your dreams. No really, this is what I thought, and we all know that this is how most people think at that age. It was a rude awakening to realize jobs didn't grow on trees, nobody had time to mentor me, and I was sorely mistaken if I thought people would know how talented I was by sitting alone in my bedroom. My confidence was at an all-time low and I felt like I wasn't just hitting a wall, the wall was slapping me in the face. It's the same wall that to this day that I sometimes run in to; the only difference is that I taught myself the tools to handle it better.

It was at that time that I decided that I was the only one responsible for my learning. So, I started reading any book I could get my hands on. If I didn't know about business plans I got a book on business plans, computers were my sworn enemy so I got Auto CAD for dummies (three times, don't laugh). I also received great advice from a friend of mine, she said my insecurities stem from my lack of knowledge, so go out there and fill in the blanks. Remember that knowledge is king. I know some people would argue that cash is king, but trust me that you have to know how to get the cash first before the cash comes. If I didn't know something I would make a note of it and research it that very night. My dad would call that tenacity, and I was in a sink or swim moment.

Exercise 2: Now write down a different list. This list will be of what you want in life. Like the big things and the small things. Don't let judgement affect what you write down. Just allow yourself to dream for a minute. Write down where you live, what does your house or even the rooms look like. Write down what you drive and who's in your life. Be as detailed as you like, and pictures or magazine cutouts would help greatly. This is your list. Now put this list somewhere that you can see it every day. It's ok to add to it and change it around as you go.

Knowing who you are will have some harsh realities that you are going to have to face. Like there may be things you don't know or need to change and improve upon. What you show the world and who you know yourself to be can be very different from one another, which is okay as long as you know your truth. So, look at yourself; look at the good, the bad, and the ugly. Once you are honest with yourself then you can start playing with different directions. Now it's one thing to not know something and quite another to look like you don't know something. I found that the saying "fake it till you make it" became my mantra. Always show up like you're not only on top of your game, you invented the game. This is not to be mistaken for being cocky, but know that your energy always enters a room before you do.

There's a story that my mom used to tell me from back in the day that always comes to mind whenever I need an extra dose of courage. To me this is the stuff that guts are made of. My dad was at his bar, when some guys from another "family" that didn't get along so well with my dad's "family" walked in. Some words were exchanged and before you knew it a fight had broken out. They worked over my dad pretty good and he could barely walk, let alone stand. By the next day everyone had heard of what happened, and in that life if someone gets one over on you, then you lose respect. And losing respect can cost you your life. Knowing this, my dad got dressed in his usual three-piece suit, cuff links, pinky ring and all. He then went back to the bar and stood in the corner, so that everyone could see that he was not only still standing, but he looked good doing it. He was battered but not broken, and he showed the world what they needed to see. An extreme example I know, but it definitely gives me a good kick in the butt when I need it!

You are always in charge of what the world sees, regardless of what you're feeling on the inside. People will feel your intentions before words are even spoken. And every thought carries with it a vibration that sends a clear message. If you come from a place of fear and insecurity, then that's what people will react to. You have to be able to visualize yourself playing a role, that of someone who has already accomplished everything that you have wanted. Don't worry if you're not there yet, you will be, and anyway they don't know that. This is also accomplishing something that is very key to your growth. If you can give your body and thoughts a glimpse of what the future feels like, then you are creating a space for your future. Our thoughts and intentions are the truth whether it's good or bad. If you feel like a failure, then that's what you'll be, but if you feel like a success, then that will be true as well. Deepak Chopra explains that the moment you have a thought or an intention, your body starts to physically prepare for that action because it isn't aware that it's not a reality. It may seem strange for me to tell Mob stories within the same pages that I speak about Deepak Chopra, but these are the beautiful layers that make up who I am.

Don't be discouraged if this doesn't come naturally to you. It all feels foreign in the beginning; the first step will be about doing it, not feeling it. As you become more comfortable going through the motions, then the emotions will match the action. I know this is not something that is taught to you as a young adult. Some people were raised in environments that this comes as second nature, to not only themselves but to their family as well. But some of us had to fight to get these attributes. Look at this as your suit of armor as you challenge a world that will always look to challenge you. Before this knowledge comes in and before the skills are learned, the only tools you have are yourself. And as time goes on, after you do learn all of the skills and knowledge that you need, you'll realize that in the end you also will only have yourself. If you have a strong sense of who you are, then no one will be able to take that away from you, unless you give it away. To trust yourself and to trust your instincts can take years to master. It's funny because it's the simplest thing you have, and it's there all along inside of you. But sometimes it's hard to hear the whisper when there's so much noise around you. Telling you who and what you should be and what your life should look like. Now don't get me wrong, it's important to try out different things. It's rare that you're born knowing exactly what you're meant to do and exactly the type of life that you're meant to live.

Whose journey are you on?

It's the unwanted roads and mistakes that show us what we don't want and will magnify what we do want. Each journey has clues and arrows to guide you in the direction you need to go. What confuses us the most is that there are so many options available to us, as well as our lack of confidence to pick one. We live in a world that there are too many options; we have so much at our disposal. It makes us very aware that by picking one option then we're saying no to all the others, and that is just plain frightening. We forget that you're allowed to change your mind, and that the point is all about following your joy. I have to constantly remind myself about this because I am one of those people who don't like to make decisions that I'm not sure of. I think it's because once I commit to something, I really commit.

If you don't feel right about the direction you're going, then change your course. There's no rule book that says you should do the same thing for the rest of your life. I'm not saying that following your passion is easy, but on the other hand you shouldn't give up after every roadblock. But if you don't feel like you're living your best life, then you have the freedom to change it. That's the beauty of freedom of choice; you can exercise it at any time.

First let your emotion guide you in the direction you want to go. Only then should you let your brain take over. Following through with action, planning and movement; all very important steps that should happen once the spark has been ignited. Going through this process will help shape and form who you will become. The process is always more important than the result. How you forged your way through the journey is the journey. The destination is just where you think you want to be right now. The whole point is wanting to be something more than what you are, and knowing you have something inside of yourself that needs to be expressed. Allow yourself the space to change your dream when you are going through all of this. Know that there will be twists and turns and ups and downs. Allow yourself to be human and accept the freedom that the journey is showing you.

This is coming from a person whose life lesson has been to live into the journey. I was never worried about what other people thought of me or how they told me to live my life. Fighting for my passion has also never been truly hard, not in the epic way I see in other people's lives. But I am a very controlled and organized person. So of course, when you want that in your life, that's when life will challenge the very aspects that make you comfortable. Just when I needed to win, I would fail. And just when I was so sure of something, it would fall apart. Sound familiar?

A few years back I stood freezing in line to audition for HGTV's Design Star. I had already sent in a video but my friends and family told me I should try out in person. I tried out never really thinking they'd choose me, and more than a little intimidated by the competition that I saw on the show. But I figured I had nothing to lose, so off I went. Well round after round of interviews I would make it through, and by the fourth round, I realized I may actually be chosen. And then it happened, I was chosen to be on season six of HGTV's Design Star! It scared the crap out of me but it was literally my dream come true. This was my chance, my shot and I just knew it was meant for me. The stars had aligned and I was going for it. Well fast forward to me being the first eliminated off the show. I know right!

I would have sworn that this was my big break. As I sat in a cold back lot of the set with my castmates, waiting to find out who was going to be the first to be eliminated, I knew it was me. It's funny because while everyone else was scared stiff, and some were just openly praying not to get sent home, a weird sort of peace came over me. I realized some really important things about myself in that moment. First, I realized that it wasn't about the show at all, it was about me. This wasn't my big moment; it was just one moment in my life. It was up to me if I was going to let it define me or refine me.

The second realization was that I had no idea what type of show I wanted to put out into the universe, and if I didn't know, then why should I be handed one. I knew what type of show HGTV wanted, and I just said the things that fit in with their model. So, it was with this moment of clarity that I walked back into the studio to get eliminated. I walked away with faith in myself, and I decided it was time I figured out just who I wanted the world to see when they looked at me.

My journey took me to the realization that the only thing I could depend on was that I would figure it out myself. You cannot build a solid ground on someone else's beliefs. When I went in a direction that was true to who I was, I always came out on top. Because my failures weren't failures, they were learning experiences to help me get to the next level. You realize that with failure, it's just an opportunity with a mask on. Sounds hokey I know, but it's so true. Because there is no one right direction, each road will take you to different possibilities. And sometimes the possibility will be more amazing than you ever thought you could dream, because you never knew how to dream so big.

If you're lucky, you allow yourself to go through many dreams. Some you'll reach and realize, "what's next?" Some you'll throw away because they're not good enough anymore or because they just don't fit who you have become. Be kind to yourself and allow the flexibility of something as simple as changing your mind. This is very hard to do if you're a person of conviction, which can be a great thing, but it's a double-edged sword. Know the difference between a failure being a mountain to overcome and when failure is the opportunity for a dream change. If you trust your instincts and relax into the journey, then your reward for letting go will be more freedoms than you could have ever imagined.

Are you hearing voices?

Now judgment is a powerful word that will cut both ways. We judge ourselves the most when deciding whether to make the popular choice or the one that will make us happy. You also have a choice when other people pass judgment on you; you can decide to accept the judgment or to ignore it. Either way it's a conscious decision you have to make.

Self-judgment or judgments that you accept as your truth will always create a space of separation. It is that space of separation that allows you to cut off your emotion from the action. Because when we judge ourselves one of two things will happen, you will either immediately become defensive, or you will believe it to be true because you haven't taken the time to look at yourself properly. Sometimes when we're defensive about something, it means we believe there's a shred of truth to what is being said. Either of these responses is saying to you that the judgment is true. But we have a third option that most people take years to realize.

The third option is to question the judgment. You have to see where the judgment is coming from. Are the voices from those we've known for years? Or are they things we've been telling ourselves for so long that we've started believing them? This goes back to who you believe you are at your very core. Judgment is a very lethal word because it makes something true in your mind. When you judge yourself in your mind there's nobody there to tell you whether that's true or false but yourself. That's why it's so lethal, because even if it's not true we have decided to make it true by thinking it. To make a judgment is to make it absolute. For instance, I can be the skinniest girl in the world but if I believe myself to be fat, then that's my truth. There's a whole other world going on inside our head and you have to be very selective of what you allow inside.

Are your thoughts just patterns that you keep propagating or are they based on reality? A lot of what we believe as our value systems has nothing to do with who we are. They have been passed onto us through family members, friends and people we grow up around. We are affected more than anything by the bubble that we live in and by the media, such as newspapers and advertisements. You have to act like the gatekeeper that only allows in what you know to be true for you. And we're no better than other people because the easiest thing to do in the world is to judge others. So, while you need to be careful about what you let inside of your brain, you have to also be just as careful as what you let out of your mouth. A separation happens when judging other people, because it puts you in an imaginary advantage over others. The result being that it's an immediate high because it makes you feel better about yourself. It doesn't last long because it is based on untruths. Worst of all, we've become the white noise for somebody else that we are at the same time trying to block out for ourselves.

I'm not saying that doing all of this is easy. Nor am I coming from a place of being like some Zen master telling you how to live your life every day. I mean judging is what I do for a living. But I try to stick to design and I try not to make it personal. I'm talking about the serious stuff, the words and thoughts that can change you. This is about trying and being the observer when you catch yourself in an inauthentic place. This is about being aware of your actions, as well as the actions you don't take. Being the observer is just stepping outside of who you are and seeing the truth. If you see something within yourself that doesn't feel right you have to become comfortable asking yourself where that action came from.

I believe when you know better it's easier to do better. If you're reading this book, it means that you want to do better; you want to live a full life, a life tailored to you personally. The words I'm telling you right now are to lay the groundwork for your life. Finding out who you are has to first start with self-awareness and grow from there. But this is just the beginning because if you're fortunate you will spend the rest of your life getting to know who you are. The growth makes the journey worth living and the ups and downs are the proof that you're alive.

CHAPTER 2

Kicking fear in the teeth

The fear will always be there, but worse than fear is regret.

So, you say you don't know what you're passionate about. Is it that you don't know what you're passionate about or are you afraid to make a passionate move? Don't confuse the two, because fear is just as strong of an emotion as passion. The only difference that will tip the scale is an emotion called courage. You need to have the courage to fail, because that is a very real possibility when you decide to create the life you want. But make no mistake about it; no move is sometimes the worst move that you can make.

What is the power of three?
The power of three is what gets you through the journey. Three being fear, courage and passion. Fear lets you know that you feel

something, because fear means you're close to hitting the mark and that there's energy. You need courage to get past the fear, and you need courage to make mistakes. Mistakes are life's way of teaching you something. And lastly you need passion to get you past the failures. Passion is the only thing that will push you through the darkness. If you knew you would succeed, then there's nothing that you wouldn't try. That's where having faith and having a plan come into play. But first you need to go in a direction for the universe help you out, that's the way life works.

If you think you can sit at home praying for the perfect life and that a salesman will come to the door and hand it to you, you're sorely mistaken. But the other side of the coin is that if you think that you alone will create the life that you want then you're equally mistaken. Creating a plan will feed the practical side of your brain, but when you create a plan with passion, well then you are empowering your life. One cannot be done without the other; it's two sides of the same coin.

I always find it funny when I hear people talk about how many ideas they have and how they would do things different if they had it their way. It's the same people who believe that it's just going to miraculously happen one day. Literally just happen, without doing anything to push it along. Successful people have one thing in common; action. You see, we are all scared but some of us decided to kick fear in the teeth and go for it anyway. That's the only difference between a successful person and a not successful person. When you are reaching for something really big in your life, and when I mean big I mean whatever your version of big is, I can guarantee you a few absolutes: one is that you should be scared witless (or else why do it) and two is that you will fail at some point.

Feeling scared and failing is all very normal. If you don't believe me ask someone you think is uber-successful, and you think somehow caught a lucky break to get where they are. In fact, tell them how lucky you think they are for being in their position and watch the look on their face very closely. If it looks anything like my face, you would see a few emotions ranging from puzzled to a bit of eye-rolling. I'm not going to lie, my friends tell me I can't hide a thing with my facial expressions. It's probably rude of me but my face is nothing if not honest. Maybe a few lifetimes ago I would have made a similar comment, but I know better now, and I have the battle wounds to prove it. You can't really blame us, and by us I'm referring to the world. You see, we are a world that showcases our accomplishments but hides our failures in the shadows. We are getting better at it; the veil is becoming more translucent but we have a ways to go.

It's one of the things that drive me. Like everyone else, all I truly want is to be seen for who I am, to be allowed to be authentic. You hope that the world accepts you for who you are failures and all. And when that doesn't always happen then you start to understand that it's you who has to accept who you are first before anyone else can.

What is the story behind the story?

It's important to learn the story behind the story, because we all have one. I have not just had failures, I have had epic failures, and I have not only been scared in my life, I have been scared frozen. My biggest fear was the one that pushed me into action. The fear of regret. What if I tried nothing, did nothing, and at the end realized I played it safe. I've seen people who have lived their whole life and became a cliché because they never fully lived life. Most people, when asked if they have any regrets, will tell you about all of the things they regretted not doing.

I have always had this voice that I hear in my head when it's time for a big leap of faith, and it started when I was young. My father died when I was twelve and my mother had remarried a very nice man who was the opposite of my father. I loved my mother but at eighteen we found ourselves butting heads. I was raised in a strict religious household for most of my childhood into my teen years and they weren't all easy years for me. My mother tried her best but I didn't exactly fit in, and while I connected with the religion, I didn't feel it was for me anymore. I felt like I had outgrown my skin and that I was wearing clothes that just didn't fit me. I've learned to recognize this feeling over the years as a sign that it's time to get out of dodge. It grows steadily stronger and stronger until I can't take it anymore and I just suddenly hit the brakes on the train and jump off. Well this was the first time I had felt this way and I knew that the only way I was going to survive and salvage a relationship with my mother was to leave home. I know this statement sounds odd but I would have done more damage if I had stayed.

This decision came to me one night after my mother and I had gotten into a fight on whether or not I was going to go to one of the meetings that evening. My mother was on the "yes you are going" end, while I was on the "don't hold your breath" end of the argument. Before she left she dramatically told me "I'm leaving and you better be there tonight or..." I can't really remember what she threatened but it was probably an "or else" or something like that. Something just snapped in me and I just knew I had to leave, leave where, I had no idea but I had to get out of there. So, I stuffed some clothes in a bag, grabbed what I could and drove off in a car I had no idea how I was going to pay for.

I didn't have a plan but I knew what I didn't want, and I knew what I wanted one day to become. The first couple of months were the hardest because when I decided to leave home I also said good-bye to the only identity I had known and goodbye to my community and any friends I knew. I was all alone and had to figure out where to go from there. I had never even washed my own clothes let alone provided for myself. I was in between jobs and needed a new one, and had to find a place to live. In the meantime, I stayed off and on with some new friends I had made and even slept in my car. A friend at the time told me that if I could make it on my own for a year then I would be fine. Well I got a job in my industry, got my own apartment and even learned how to do my own laundry. Oh, and in case you wanted to know, my mother is to this day my best friend and we're like two peas in a pod.

I think it's important to understand that now is the time you need to take hold of your life and figure out when you want it to begin. Sometimes it's more important to go in a direction, than to know exactly where you're going to end up. This is an area where you need to use emotion as your guidepost and leave your brain out of it, for now. Would you want to do it if you had all of the support and perfect circumstances to support you? These are the questions that you should be asking yourself. You are the only one who con-trols your life and destiny. When I was a little girl I used to day-dream while starring out the window of my parents' car. I dreamt of being something bigger than anything I had knowledge about. I wanted to be someone who felt alive and passionate about what my life was. I'm also pretty sure I wanted to be a rock star (you never know it could still happen), but as we get older our dreams change, shift, and if we're lucky, they grow.

Exercise 3: I want you to take the list you made of what you want in life and next to each item that you listed, write down the worst-case scenario of what could happen if you went for it and it didn't work out. Really look at the worst-case scenarios of what could happen and read them out loud. I find that when you say your fears out loud then they lose some of their hold on you. Now next to the worst-case scenarios, write down what you would do next. Do you just wither and die after the worst-case scenario happens, or can you visualize how you would handle it and move on? Can you close your eyes and put yourself in that situation and feel the energy of the freedom you would feel once you realized that the worst had happened, but that you were still standing?

I came to design because I loved the arts but as my mother put it "you'll starve as an artist, so pick something you can make money at with your art." This did not come off as harsh to me; it came off as realistic at the time. I loved any form of art as long as I could draw and sketch. To me there are so many outlets to what we can do and how we can express ourselves that there never is just one right answer, just an answer that feels right. The only wrong direction is when it feels so inauthentic to who you are that you find yourself watching your life like a movie that's stuck on pause. If I had the confidence I would have insisted I become an artist, but I felt it in my bones that she was right. Of course, when I then informed her that I wanted to be an Interior Designer she answered in her usual Latin accent and over-expressive face (which I have inherited, the over-expressive face that is) "really, Interior Design? You know that's as hard as breaking into modeling."

Now that advice didn't deter me one bit because Interior Design felt right to me. You need to know when to take advice and when to make decisions based on what fits for you. She was right that going into Interior Design was as hard as breaking into model-ing, but she didn't know something that I knew. I had a passion for design and that passion would see me through the hard times. That and the fact that once I set my mind to something, I'd rather chew off my arm than give up on it (sorry for the graphic example). I was too young to have a fear of what I was undertaking (I was only 16-years old when I made this huge revelation), as most kids are. So, I had the two out of three; passion and courage, but they are the best odds you have sometimes. You see, people will put their own limitations on you, not because they don't want you to succeed but because they couldn't imagine taking on the challenge themselves. Tell me a dream you have and I'll tell you a million reasons why it won't or can't work. That's why the passion needs to be sparked.

What does fear look like to you?

Don't be discouraged if your passion feels more like a tea light and less like a forest fire, it will get there. It's hard to get a good fire going when there's so much brain chatter going on, white noise as I call it. The fear will always be there, but worse is the fear of not going for it. I still feel it to this day. Sometimes it disguises itself as the easy road or on other days it's my busy life that gives me the perfect excuse not to tackle a new and exciting venture. Fear doesn't always look the same and it changes its tactics as you catch on to its slick ways. Fear is a shameless pair of shady boots!

I'm speaking to you as someone who has walked through the fire and is on the other side. This is not to say that I don't have many more fires to walk through, but those will have their own set of unique challenges. There is a duality that creates the life that you want. Two worlds have to become one; in other words, your emotion has to connect with an action. I can wax on all day till I'm blue in the face of what your intentions need to be, but without action you'll get nowhere. Putting pen to paper and connecting with people are what get you to the other side. Passion is just passion without a plan, but a passionate plan gives you the life you were meant to live. I know this all sounds like major B.S. but I am living proof that this really works.

I think that sometimes we think that first step is a lot harder than it needs to be because we turn it into this big dark mountain. I think it's our natural instinct. It's definitely something I do all the time. In fact, I have to constantly teach myself not to do it. It's the feeling like you're stepping on the edge of a cliff and you catch your breath, because you don't know what's on the other side. That feeling is always there and it will always be there. The more times you step off the cliff, the more you realize that there is nothing to worry about. You never really took a fall, you just stepped into another journey. I guess it's the fear of the unknown that paralyzes us. It's our own voice in which we tell ourselves "what if this is the best I'll ever be?"

or "what if I don't achieve what I set out to do?" Even writing this book took a lot of courage for me to start to write at all.

All the noise that kicks up as soon as I sit in front of my computer can be debilitating. And my own voices are one thing, but if I had a dollar for every publisher and editor that rejected me I'd be driving that Mercedes I have my eye on. As a career my life has always been design, and in the book and TV world, once you are known as someone who is aligned with an idea, then that is the box that you are placed in and that is the box in which they would like you to stay. Why? Because it's proven to work and they have a platform in which to build upon. Because that is a horse that they can bet on, one everyone knows. They know how the world will receive it and you, because the world already has. They don't know what to do with an Interior Designer who wants to write about design, energy, motivation, her life, and connecting all of the dots that make up who we are.

You name it and I've heard it! I'm too cheeky and sarcastic to sit on a shelf next to Deepak Chopra. I don't have enough training to motivate people and be placed in the self-help section. God forbid I end up in the biography section; I'm only in my 30's. I haven't lived enough. They would love to place me and my book in the design section, if I could just fall into line and stop writing about life and energy, and add more pretty pictures to the book. I mean after all, isn't that what I'm known for. You get the idea. Every new dream and direction comes with its very own set of fears and potential road blocks.

These are really the questions that stop us from going in a direction. It's not the lack of direction, it's the fear of stepping out of our comfort zone and ending up worse off than where we started, because that would mean we have failed and made a mistake. And the belief is if that happened then our world would cease to exist. This couldn't be farther from the truth and you know it. We all really know it. We just choose to ignore the reality. The reality is that we are stronger than we give ourselves credit for. Its life's situations that push us into experiences that therefor forces us to stand in our own strength.

When we fail, our life doesn't crumble, that's our fear talking. We are actually being given the opportunity to metamorphose. It's a gift that most people rarely see because they're afraid to take the chance to fail. And those who have been given this gift yearn for the opportunity to have the mirror held up to themselves once again. My biggest growth time is after I thought I hit bottom and had nowhere to go. The beauty of what happens next, if you remain open to it, is that you have released all of the old ways of trying to solve it. You are left with no other choice than to take a different path, one that you may have ignored because you were so set in your ways. But a new path can bring unexpected blessings.

When you decide to take a chance, or go in a direction, what you're really saying is "I believe in me," because you have no one to fall back on but yourself. It's the belief that no matter what is thrown at you or where you may fall, you will depend on yourself to come through it. No one ever goes into this having full faith in themselves. So if you think that's what you'll need to get started, you're fooling yourself. This is something that you'll learn along the way. This faith in yourself will get built with each small victory. Things you wouldn't normally notice like the first time you voiced your passion. To someone else this may seem small, but you felt the difference. Do not lie to yourself or discount what you feel to be true.

That feeling of your heart skipping a beat was a step in the right direction. That was a sign telling you to "go this way." That was a building block toward your faith in yourself. You are connecting into the flow of your rightful energy. People think that the signs are supposed to be big and just smack you in the head. Not to say that at times it doesn't happen that way, but don't be so quick to dismiss the small signs.

CHAPTER 3

Creating a passionate plan

Dreams that turn into plans are called goals.

know that the idea of making a plan sounds very rudimentary and old-fashioned, but trust me it's not. It's the very staple that turns dreams into realities. Granted you need drive and perseverance, but without a plan you're just shooting missiles in the dark. I know, plans scare people because if there's a plan it means there is black and white proof of success or failure. But it's literally not that black and white. Plans are not just made up of the big milestones, but are more importantly made up of the smaller steps that need to happen before a big milestone is ever reached. If you look at any situation as a whole, it's seems like a large scary monster. I know, because I've psyched myself out in the past with that type of thinking. It's all in your head. You can really do a number on yourself thinking over and over about this big idea that surely will be too hard, take too long, or will never happen. But that's the secret: there are tons of big ideas, people have them all of the time. The only difference with achieving them is that they were broken down into manageable steps. Getting out of your own way is the biggest obstacle to overcome.

And I don't mean when it's easy and all the doors are opening for you. I mean when all you're hitting are road blocks. You have to make a conscious decision to shut the voices out, especially your own. You alone get to decide what you will let become your belief system. People can talk and things can happen to you, but will you accept them as your truth? That is a decision only you can make.

How does the Plan come together?

Exercise 4: Let's get back to the plan. Even if you don't believe it will help you, it won't hurt to make one. Everyone will have different ways that will work for them, so feel free to tweak this to your situation. I am just simply filling you in on what's worked for me. Grab a pencil and paper or you can use your computer or IPad. You're going to need your lists from the previous chapters that you had put aside. It's time to explore what tackling some of those dreams would realistically look like. Again, don't freak out, we are just dreaming on paper right now, without any judgments. Look at your list from Exercise 3 titled "Life Wants" that showed the worst-case scenarios. Highlight the "Life Wants" that still resonated with you even after you wrote the worst-case scenario next to them. These are the dreams that have more of a fighting chance to make it.

Let's get started! At the top of the page, write down the name you'd like to call your plan, but give it some juice and have fun with it. Please don't just write down the word plan, it's the quickest way to make sure you stay uninspired. For instance; "My Shut Up and Do It Plan" or "My Emergency Plan" (sounds dramatic, but isn't your life in a state of emergency?). You get the idea. You need a title that literally screams at you whenever you glance at it. Next write down your goals next to one another, and leave room below each goal heading. Guess what, you can write down as many as you want. This isn't a term paper that you're handing in—this is your life. Go big or go home!

Now, below each goal heading write down the steps you think you would need to take to reach each goal. It's okay if this first draft looks messy and scribbly. You can turn it into a clean version afterwards. Use this version as your very own think tank. Now take a look at all of the goals and the supporting steps that you wrote down, and I want you to write something simple that you can do each day to reach the steps that you need to take. It can be something simple that takes a few minutes during lunch, like online research or reaching out to someone who could help you reach your goals. Sometimes you feel like you're stuck and that you have no control over your future. But I have always found that there is always something small that you can do that will not only help you to progress, but will keep you motivated enough till you get to the larger goals.

I was recently looking at a plan that I wrote about twelve years ago (and yes, I keep my journals and plans). It reminds me of how far I've come, which gives me the steam I need to make new plans. Also, the great thing about reaching all of your goals is that you get to make new ones. Anyway, my plan had everything from saving $10,000 in the bank, being on TV, to going to the gym consistently. If I wanted it, it went on the list. I remember the first list I ever wrote had the goal "make enough money to buy myself one new shirt a month". I was very focused on that, since I didn't have two nickels to rub together. My steps for my one shirt a month goal was to set career goals that would bring in additional income. That was the larger steps that I needed to take. But I could take daily steps that were in my power to make. I decided to make my pricey coffee at home every morning, and save that money to put toward my little shopping trip.

It seems so small, but my daily small tasks made me feel in control of my destiny and kept me going until I could make more money. The same can be said for even the larger goals; like my goal for being on TV. My steps looked something like: send in my application to TV shows; build my resume to be someone that a TV network would even look at; build a kick ass website (believe it or not it's how most producers find you and how the rest will vet you); and network with people who could help me to reach my goal. My daily tasks started out with researching TV networks looking for Interior Designers, researching website ideas that would inspire me for my own, and attending networking events where I could meet new people. Now I want to explain how taking these actions got me the results that I wanted, but in two very different ways.

My first TV appearance I was on was HGTV's Design Star, and I achieved this by directly submitting my tape and by going to an open casting call. They loved my personality and experience, and they also loved my website. My preparation really helped support my action of showing up to play ball. The second TV show Travel Channel's Hotel Impossible came about very differently. It actually all started before I ever stepped foot on HGTV. I got a call out of nowhere from a producer in New York, who told me that they came across my website and bio and loved it. They wanted to know if they could shoot a sizzle reel with me to pitch to networks for a TV show. For all of you who have no idea what a sizzle reel is, it's a short commercial that runs about five minutes or less that gives a network a sneak peek into what your TV show would look like.

I of course agreed thinking this was my lucky break and that of course it was going to be a success. So what, I had no idea what kind of show I wanted to do! Next thing I knew I was filming with a bunch of strangers for what felt like the most boring sizzle reel I'm sure was ever created. Ok let's dial it back, I'm sure there have been worse but I didn't get a call back so I'm sure I wasn't going to win any awards. By the way, I just thought that it was a one-time thing that I didn't get a return phone call once they knew that my show wasn't getting picked up. I have since learned that this rudeness runs all across every production company I have ever come across. Just a side note to any production companies reading this— it only takes a few seconds to be polite.

My life went on and about a year later I tried out for Design Star, made it on and was voted off. The story is old news to you by now. You would think that Hotel Impossible came out of my Design

Star appearance, but nope not at all. It must have been six or so months after Design Star, and about two years after my first sizzle run-in with the New York production company, that they came knocking again. They were shooting a new hotel renovation show and they needed a local Interior Designer to do an episode, and they remembered me from the sizzle reel I did with them. Would I be interested, and if so, could I get on a plane in two days. No seriously, that's how the conversation went. One amazingly grueling show turned into five seasons and you know the rest.

The reason I say that Hotel Impossible was a different avenue is because it wasn't a result of a direct action. Yes, it helped that I had a great website so that they could initially find me. But the first try tanked and I thought I'd never hear from them again. I truly believe that the energy I created by consistently going in the direction of my dream is really what in the end brought my dream right to my doorstep. Sometimes you think that your actions are futile and a waste of time, but it's a proven fact that whatever you concentrate on will grow. It may not happen exactly when you think it should happen but it will happen when it's ready to. You may think I'm crazy but it's not my law, it's universal law. For instance, it's like when you're car shopping and you decide on the make and model of the car that you know is the one you want to buy. Now think about how many times a day you ended up seeing that exact car everywhere you go. I'm giving you a simple example, but it's true all the same.

Never has a statement been truer that the journey is just as important as the destination. It's not as simple as making a plan, it's taking the time to write it out, update it, put energy into it and out into the world. Every time you take a small step, you are telling the universe that this is what you want and what you deserve. Now I want you to take this plan a step further and imagine for at least five minutes before you go to sleep that you already have everything on your list of ultimate goals. It all has to go together; the plan, the energy, and the imagination. Remember when you were a kid and you daydreamed about being a rock star, an astronaut, or a cowboy. It all seemed so real, and you could imagine every detail; what you were wearing and what you were doing. It's that pure daydreaming that you need to tap into now. As we get older we lose our capability to daydream, we fill the time with schedules and to do lists. Which are important, don't get me wrong. But it's the daydream that feeds the soul, makes us believe it's possible. You see your body and the universe don't know that it's not real. They react as if what you're seeing and feeling is very real, and will act accordingly. The pleasure endorphins that get released when you daydream about something that makes you happy are the same, if not better, when you work out or have a good laugh.

Planning and lists have always excited me because I'm a girl who likes to take action. I love the daydream and the ideas part of it all, but as soon as I get excited about an idea I want to get started, like yesterday. I always post my plan in plain view, either by my desk or on my fridge. I urge you to do the same. It doesn't matter where, just as long as you can see it every day. You need to see it, to let it fuel the fire in you. It can't do that buried away in some drawer. Take it one step further and write down your immediate daily action steps on a post-it note, and stick it on your computer or in your wallet. We are a species that in today's busy society needs reminders before something becomes second nature. You have to implement it and make it part of your daily life in order for it to work!

CHAPTER 4

When in doubt kick it out

You don't own stuff, it owns you.

The negative is just as important as the positive. This means that every space doesn't need to be filled with stuff and clutter. This is both true for your physical space as well as for your non-physical space. Let's take the non-physical first, because I believe that is where the clutter starts. Purposeful space leaves room for growth and inspiration. Some call it meditation while others just call it being. Whatever label you give it doesn't change the fact that it's a pure necessity. Every day our mind gets taken up with what I call white noise; the thoughts of others, the rules of your parents, the pressures of the media, and worst of all, your own self-criticism.

The problem with this chatter is that when you actually need the space to process where you stand and who you are, there isn't any. It's a constant hamster wheel that fools you into thinking that if you're not thinking and problem-solving, nothing will get done. This is the farthest thing from the truth. It's a lie! You just keep obsessing because you (and when I say you I mean me too) have this constant need to fix it and to control the outcome. It's less scary that way. Controlling the situation makes us feel safe, having all of the answers makes us feel safe. And so it takes internal strength to handle space. Because once we make room for it, sometimes it takes everything you've got, not to try to clutter it up again with crap.

The truth is that a lot of the voices that are in your head aren't real, and most of your problems will never be solved with the same thought process that got you there in the first place. We are programmed to worry, and when we have nothing to worry about, we worry about that too. Yet it would be overly simplifying it if I told you to just clear your mind and all will be better. What I will say is that I have learned to become the watcher of my thoughts, because I didn't like some of the moods that resulted when I let my mind wonder.

Who's doing the leading?

For example, when I was a teenager I used to tell my mother that I was depressed, to which she would reply "you're just bored, go do something with yourself." The reason I would think that I was depressed was because I would listen to a new song on the radio, which usually was about some lost or angry love, and I would start thinking about a love that was lost to me. Actually, it was probably more like a boy that I thought was cute that never eveeeeer gave me the time of day. But by the end of the song I was pretty sure that he was the love of my life and that I was just as hopeless as the girl on the radio. In fact, the more I thought about it, I was pretty sure he didn't like me because I was horrible at math and had braces (and pimples, but that's another story). By the time I was done going over and over it in my head, I was convinced I'd never get married, my friends never liked me anyway, and I was dumb as rocks. No really, this was the path my brain followed. If you think about the last time you got upset by something or someone, I'll bet you came away from it with a few stories of your own.

I did a great job of twisting my family's words, reading into friends' silences, and pretty much assuming the worst of a situation. And it all started with one little song that was probably written by a happily married song writer in LA making a ton of cash. Your mind is a powerful tool, and it may be hard to control the thoughts that float in and out of it, but you can control what thoughts you allow to take up permanent space. And you are always in control of what thoughts you decide to kick out. I use the term kick out because these are not harmless thoughts that one day you hang out with and the next day you put on the shelf.

These are mind invaders that when left alone will control your life. So you have to use the same attitude you would use when kicking out an ex-boyfriend. Be aware of your triggers. Since I became aware of the sappy songs that send me into an emotional roller coaster, I now choose to change the station. Why listen to a sad song when a happy one leaves me feeling.... well, happy.

Another mental vampire as I like to call them, are the problems that never have solutions. Some of them actually do have solutions, but you keep using the same problem-solving tactics to solve them, so you essentially never reach a new conclusion. You need to just stop and pull the plug; just let your mind fade to black. I recommend meditation, it has helped me tremendously. But before you start freaking out because you've tried meditation and it doesn't work for you, give me a minute to explain.

You think that in order to meditate you need to go into lotus position and clear your mind for hours while monks chant in the background. Not true. Meditation can mean different things to different people, and it's unique to everyone. You just have to find your groove. I tried it for years and I couldn't do it. My mother doesn't believe in it, but she believes in prayer, and guess what, that's a form of meditation. Anything that stops you from thinking about the past, worrying about the future, and brings you back to the present, is a form of meditation.

I realized about five years ago that I actually had the tools to quiet my mind all along; it was the same tools that negatively affected me when I was younger. Like I mentioned earlier, I loved music and I had and still have a very overactive imagination. This, as a side note, serves me better as a designer then as an overly dramatic teenager. Anyway, I digress; I attended a seminar where they had us get into a circle on the floor to teach us a form of meditation. I proceeded to take my place even though I kept telling myself silently that it wasn't going to work, since every time I closed my eyes I saw utility bills and to do lists. But since I am always on the quest for self-awareness and expansion, I kept an open mind.

I waited for the silence, literally, and that's when I heard the music, again literally. It was beautiful and not like the boring stuff that you hear during yoga, but it held energy and invited you to use your imagination. That's when the instructor started to speak. Again, I had never attended a speaking meditation and I was surprised. She encouraged us to use our imagination and to visualize a space or time that made us happy. Even if it was make-believe, it didn't matter because our thoughts made it real. I imagined lush landscapes where flowers bloomed and unicorns flew in the sky. I imagined that I was safe and warm, and that everywhere I walked, I was surrounded by light that danced all over me from above.

Before I knew it twenty minutes had passed and the music had ended, and we were being told to open our eyes. When I did I was both sad to say goodbye to my utopia, and at the same time I had never felt so relaxed and present. I couldn't believe that not even one utility bill had flashed before my eyes! I also realized one of the most important lessons I will ever learn—I realized that those minutes gave me true perspective. All of the worries and thoughts I had before now seemed so petty and insignificant. They weren't as important as I had given them credit for. The more power I gave to the space I had created, took the power away from the worries I had. Some of the problems that were obviously real were still there but I somehow now knew that over thinking wasn't going to solve them, it was just going to create more anxiety.

Now I'm sure there were others in the seminar that felt like this didn't work for them. They had to find a way to be present that would work for them. Some people go for a drive, others read, and some people play an instrument to find their center. None of these methods are wrong; they are just different methods that can take you to the same place. The clearing creates space for the right answers to come to you, but it also creates space for you to just be. It introduces new energy and changes things up. When you kick out the bad stuff, you create more opportunity for all the good stuff.

How much is too much?

Now you're probably wondering what this has to do with the clutter in your house, but I say show me a cluttered mind and I will show you a cluttered house. Now I'm not saying that this is true for everyone, but it's true for most people. Clutter means security to a lot of people. Even if it's all junk, it makes you feel like you're not alone, and if you're not alone then you're not lonely. It's interesting that I can see it so clearly when I look back over my own home living history. My first apartment was horrible. In fact, my first batch of apartments were horrible. Before I go further, I moved around like a gypsy, but blame my addiction on Interior Design. I mean why re-decorate when I can move into a shiny new apartment to clutter it all up again. Anyway, looking back on my early design years I can only describe my style as Puerto Rican 90's not-chic. If it was velvet, burgundy, or faux finished it was for me. Not to mention my addiction to dried flowers, fabric tassels, and snow globes. I guess when you tell your friends that you like snow globes expect to get one on every occasion. I had holiday snow globes, house warming snow globes, and the "I'm so sorry you and your boyfriend broke up" snow globe.... that's a true statement.

Every time that I moved I just shuffled my mountain of junk from one place to another. Half the time I didn't even like the stuff but I was sure that I needed all of it. But we all know that I didn't. See, the thing with having a lot of stuff is that it feels heavy, not only visually but emotionally too. It's one of those sneaky things that you never realize is happening until one day you wake up and realize that every nook and cranny of floor or wall space is all filled up. Now this not only applies to those of us who have accumulated a bunch of stuff. This sentiment applies to those of us who may have a few things in our space that just doesn't feel right.

The more aware I became of clearing out what didn't belong in other parts of my life, the more aware I was of needing more space in my home as well. I mean after all, if my house is where I came to relax after the stresses of my day. then it would make sense that my house shouldn't stress me out too. Let me tell you that there is no higher high that you will get then when you get rid of the stuff that you no longer need. I mean it's a serious addiction. I had no idea how great it would feel. I suddenly had space to breathe, emotionally and visually as well. I felt calmer and more organized, just plain ready to wake up and get my day started. I never realized until that moment how much all of that stuff was weighing me down. I know you know what I'm talking about because you must have gotten some glimpse of that feeling when you did your spring cleaning, or even got rid of some old clothes that no longer fit.

As I mentioned earlier, it doesn't have to be a complete overhaul. It could literally be a few items that you see every day as you walk past them on your way out the door that just isn't working for you anymore. Sometimes it could even be a piece of furniture that you inherited that you hate, but you felt pressured into taking because of sentimental value. But you hate it so why keep it when someone else could love it. I am not telling you to toss all valuable items into the trash, ok some items. But there are plenty of organizations and people who could use what you see as junk. Not to mention all of the avenues available now to sell your stuff and make some side cash. People are always surprised when they come over to my house. One reason is because it's so airy and open. I think they expect every square inch to be over designed. But I am in my clients' heads every day, jumping from one design genre to another. The last thing I want to do is be greeted by more stuff when I come home. Instead I want space to breathe and relax, and I want to be surrounded by things that make me feel happy and comfortable. This could mean different things to different people, but at the end of the day the message is still the same "when in doubt kick it out."

Exercise 5: I want you to get a sticky pad (make sure it's spanking brand new) and go room by room in your house or apartment and put a post-it note on all of the items that you don't either use, can't stand, or just plain doesn't feel right. Don't over think it; it's not like as soon as you slap a sticky note on it, it will get sucked out the front door. And FYI if you've used a whole pad in one room then you don't just need to de-clutter, you may need a complete design overhaul. Next I want you to sleep on it. Don't do a thing until you've had a good night sleep, and in the morning take a good look around and see if you still feel the same way. Don't be discouraged if your first response is to rip all of the sticky notes off of everything and plop in front of the TV. Remember

that all great changes take some big sacrifices, plus you have my word that you're going to feel better afterwards. Realistically I know that only 60% of your post-it note items will make it onto the "kick out" list, and that's ok. Your list can have anything on it from old papers, books, dishes, or furniture. Nothing is too small or too great to kick out. If it no longer serves you, you no longer need to hold onto it. A good rule of thumb moving forward is for every new item that you bring into the house, you kick an old one out. It'll keep you honest!

CHAPTER 5

The after effects

I can't feel what I don't allow in my life.

Who you are is what you surround yourself with. Those words are an understatement. It's a belief system as old as time, ingrained into the teachings of Feng Shui for instance. In modern terms, you'll see it in the philosophy of color therapy and on TV shows that focus on topics of home organization and hoarding. Even though I like to design for my clients using a lot of the teachings of Feng Shui, one of the problems I have with it is that it's taking on the ideology of someone else's belief system. There are some basics that Feng Shui teaches that are very true across the board for everybody. I like to call these teachings common sense; like allow clear space for you to breathe and live, and to always allow natural light to flow. Another theory which I am also well versed in, and it has been around since the early 60s, is sustainable design. Sustainable design is something that enriches anybody's life. The value of implementing things like proper lighting and using your local natural resources will always be beneficial to anybody who implements them. While I see the benefits to a lot of these philosophies and I utilize them within my own home, the one thing that will beat these philosophies is the acknowledgment of the person who will be enjoying the space.

There's a reason a lot of these philosophies work, and it's because they make sense for most people. What I love about Feng Shui is that it not only talks about negative and positive energy but that it's also possible to tailor it to the individual experiencing the space. Its focus is on nature and connecting yourself with those natural surroundings. It's very hard to go wrong when your focus is on natural light, natural elements, organic artwork, and a balance for your overall space. I find that most people are drawn to Feng Shui because it delves into your personality traits in a sense. It takes your birthday and the coordinates for where you were born, and even the time you were born to dictate what your space should be like. On the flip side, the problem I have with Feng Shui is that it can only take you so far. It doesn't take into account the emotions of the individual experiencing the space. Similarly, green design, color therapy, and even reorganizing your space can only take you so far as well.

Does your design empower you?

I can use all of these tools to tell you what your space will look like, and for the most part other than taking some information and some facts, I can totally eliminate you from the process. What's missing in the above philosophies is that YOU are missing from the equation. Don't get me wrong, I feel like all of these philosophies do make up the best part of what makes up design. But I also feel that whatever you give power to, whatever you believe in, is what will be true for you. So, if you have total faith in Feng Shui, then that will become a true way of life. But there's no getting away from the fact that if I revise your space using the Feng Shui method and it told me to paint your front door red, but you hate red, then you're always going to hate opening your front door. The same goes for sustainable design and color therapy. In color therapy, a color like lavender is supposed to be soothing and relaxing. But if lavender reminds you of a classroom that you hated being in as a child, then it will have the opposite effect on you. You can probably see where I'm going with this.

We are all different and we all have different types of triggers, so then no two designs should ever be alike. All of these methods can take you about 70% of the way, but they cannot complete the picture. You as the individual need to be part of the process. There's not just one boilerplate template for design that everyone gets assigned to. Yes, I can come up with an amazing design for anybody but I can't guarantee that they will feel comfortable within the space without going deeper. What you surround yourself with every day and what you wake up to will influence how you live your life more than you know. How many of you have fond memories as a child about the house you grew up in, or you may have had bad memories that affect you to this day. I can't tell you how many people's home decor makes me feel truly sad because the children are growing up in spaces that are not uniquely their own. I was called to design a home where the little girl was living in a bedroom that had the previous little boy's decor. When I asked the parents how long they had been living in the home, they told me five years. I was blown away! I doubt they had ever considered the emotional ramifications of their little girl living in a little boy's room for five years. And if you have wonderful memories of growing up in a princess room then you'll understand that this little girl's memories will never be the same. I'm not suggesting to blow the college fund on a princess room by any means. Some simple changes like fresh paint, new bed sheets, and a couple of decorations, and you would end up with a room that felt more like home to her.

We touched a little bit on this in the last chapter, but now I want to get more into how the stuff you keep around does affect you. I once had a client who felt depressed whenever they were in their own home. When I noticed a bunch of antiques in the home and had asked about them, I was told that they were from their deceased mother—heirlooms you would say. The problem is that my client didn't get along with their mother and was constantly told that their life just wasn't up to par. I suggested that they donate, give away, or even sell most of the items that belonged to their mother, and keep one piece of the inherited furniture. I don't think this even occurred to them because the antiques were in good condition, and were beautiful. And by the way, isn't it sacrilegious to give away your dead mother's furniture? Just saying!

This thought process would make sense to most people except for the ones who felt miserable every time they came home. It's not always about what makes sense or what everybody else thinks. It's about what feels right (or wrong) to you. Your home, your office, and anywhere that you spend the majority of your time should be a space that supports where you're going in life, and especially where you are in life at this very moment. That's why I believe all of it is connected and creates what I call "Empowered Design." It's about designing the life you want from the inside out, but it has to start from the inside and work its way out, not the other way around. Your space is a direct reflection and connection to who you are. There has to be a synergy involved when creating the life that you want and the space that you spend 24-hours of your day in.

It is not impossible to re-design your life and your space so that they are connected to you and who you are, so that it fuels you on a daily basis for the future that you want and deserve. We are in a new day and age where we are seeing this connection more and more. We do not live our lives in a one tonal reality. Our lives are multi-faceted and our eyes are more open to the fact that there is a design for everything we do. It's all about the individual, not about the masses. The butterfly effect teaches us that if you change one small thing then you will create change on the other side of the world. The same principles can be applied to your own life. Make the small changes in your daily life and you will change the life that you live. This is why it's important to figure out who you are first or at least the starting point of who you are. Because if you don't dive in and figure out the simple things, then it'll affect how you shape the world around you. If you look through foggy glasses, then your view of the world will be distorted.

Does it feel right?

Spiritual teachers will tell you to disconnect from everything around you, to release your attachment to the material world. This is true because the material things that we hold tightly to do not define us, they can come and go in the span of a breath. I believe that the other side of the coin is that what we surround ourselves with will affect us to our very core. We are human beings, so what we see connects us to how we feel. When I walk into a room I feel the space before I register what the room looks like. We do this automatically, it's a natural reflex. In today's society, we're becoming more comfortable saying things like, "I feel this way in the space" or "the energy of the space," etc. Sometimes you can't put your finger on it, but you know when something feels off in a room. You can tell when a room feels welcoming or when it feels cold. In both scenarios, the room can be beautifully decorated, but since each experience is individual, you are the person experiencing it. You're going to run into this all the time in the vast world of public spaces, because there are thousands of people experiencing each space at different times. This is a more critical situation that needs to be addressed when it comes to your own space, and it's your own home that feels negative or positive.

This is at the very core of what I believe to be true. And it's not just a belief system based on pure thoughts and ideas. I've seen the evidence of it time and time again in my own work and in my everyday life. And what I have learned I have applied to every part of my life, and so can you. It's the reason why this book had to encompass all of it for it to be an honest message. Granted, the message also includes my sideways humor, but I can only deliver it in my own way. The connection between it all is so clear, and if you would just allow for the possibility that what and who you surround yourself with, what you tell yourself, and that the space that you call home can have the power to diminish or empower you, then the awareness alone is enough to build upon.

It's easy to just address what you can see and feel; like furniture, paint etc., but then you would be missing the bigger picture. I'm not the kind of person that does things half way; I want to go big, and dream big. You need to be ruthless in the pursuit of your best life and use all the tools that are at your disposal. There are no do-overs in this life and you can't hit the rewind button. I ask you to take an honest snapshot of your life and to not only see what's going on but to feel what's going on, and if you don't like it then have the courage to change it.

CHAPTER 6

Finding your authentic space

Surround yourself with things that you love, and you'll never go wrong.

The principle belief that what you surround yourself with will tell you more about yourself than anything else is the same principle that needs to be applied to your personal space. Connecting yourself to your environment is one of the most important things that you'll ever do, because it has a far-reaching effect on your life. One of the hardest things to do is to get past the rules of how you're supposed to live that never actually came from your own brain. One of the ways to cut through the white noise is to catch yourself when it's only you in there, and none of the other judgment and scenarios that cloud your thoughts. You can do this by closing your eyes and meditating in the space -- seeing what comes to you and feel the energy of how you connect to your space.

It's usually how I come to a design for my own clients, especially when it doesn't come to me right away. Meditating within a space allows space for the room to speak to you. This may be hard for most people. So, the second thing I am recommending may come a bit easier.

Are you dreaming?

Exercise 6: Keep a pad and pencil next your bed and before you go to sleep I want you to say to yourself that you are open to feeling free within your space. Also, ask yourself what would make you feel the most comfortable in your surroundings. There are no hard or fast rules to this, so you can think about or ask yourselves any questions that you feel will relate to you and will help you to visualize what your space could be. This is the part that will require a little fun visualization on your part. You have to pretend that there is no budget, there are no limitations, and it also doesn't matter whether you have restrictions, because you lease or because you share your home with somebody else.

I only want you to play with these thoughts for about 5 to 10 minutes before you go to bed. You shouldn't feel any pressure, and this isn't something you should take too seriously. This is all about the fantasy of what you surround yourself with if there were no limits. I find that this is easier for children than it is for adults. As adults, we are more used to knocking down our hopes and dreams before we have a chance to dream them.

The next morning, pause right before you open your eyes, right when you're aware that it's a new day, and ask yourself what your space says to you. I want you to write down the answers no matter what comes to you, no matter if you say unicorns and rainbows or fireflies and the color blue. In those few minutes when we just wake up in the morning, before we're aware that the day has taken hold of us, there is a space that is very precious. It's the closest you'll ever get to your core emotion because it's free of judgment, and it's free of other people's restrictions. We're still caught in the dream and the essence of sleep, and are not fully aware that we're awake yet. So our dreams and our fantasy are more real to us than our daily reality. In fact, our dreams are the reality.

Sometimes I wonder which one is more real, the dream or the life that happens in between the dreaming. Either way, the jewels that you can glean from your thoughts during this time are clues to who you are and what you want. What you have done is that you have created an intention before you went to sleep, and while you slept your brain manifested answers to your questions. Sometimes you'll notice that you had dreams related to your questions or just thoughts that popped into your head as you were waking up. Don't feel discouraged if the dreams or the thoughts had nothing to do with the questions you asked. Believe it or not, the words that you wrote down are connected to the questions that you put out the night before. Our mind sometimes plays tricks on us and so this is the place where you have to become a little bit of a detective. Take the clues you have and play a game of word association. This process is personal, so the answers have to come from you, not from anybody else.

For instance, if the word butterfly popped into your brain when you woke up, then take a minute and think about what butterflies mean to you. The traditional meaning of butterflies is transformation or metamorphosis. This could mean that you're looking to transform your space into something completely different. But since this is about you, you have to think about what butterflies would mean to you. Most people I know when they think of butterflies they think of beauty, so maybe you're looking to surround yourself with beautiful things. Maybe it goes deeper than that for you. Maybe it reminds you of a field you used to play in a child. If it did, and during that time you felt free running and playing in the warmth of the sun, then this may be a reminder telling you this is how you wish to feel again.

You get the idea of how this goes. I find this to be not only a fun process but also very enlightening in figuring out things about yourself that you never really knew. Remember that how we rationalize in our waking life is not necessarily how we rationalize in our subconscious mind. That's why this is such an insightful exercise; it gives you clues to what lies behind the curtain. You would get very different answers if you sat in front of a friend and they asked you what you want your space to look like. You would immediately start thinking about the different magazines that you read and all of the various TV shows about celebrity homes. Maybe you would be influenced by the friend sitting right in front of you. For instance, if she loves nature and was big into sustainable design, then you may feel guilty telling her that you would love silk from overseas draped throughout your house. Not very sustainable, but I bet it'd make for a fabulous room!

Are you using a life label maker?

The ego plays a big role into how we live our life. We are so influenced by how we think our life should look according to the world and other people's standards, that we forget to think about how our life should feel. That's why the most important starting point of this whole process is finding that clear space where only we exist. I find that when we can quiet our mind, all sorts of answers will come to us. It's when we overthink things that we hit roadblocks. Trust me, this is something that I have to constantly remind myself of. What we're talking about can't be categorized into sections, because the moment you put labels on who you are or what you specifically like, then you are essentially cutting off opportunities for the possibility of something different.

We, as a society, are used to labels. They make us feel safe and comfortable. I see it every day in Interior Design. When I ask people what they feel their style is, I can almost guarantee you that they will say something like, "modern" or "classic." Now this may be a great starting point, as well as a way to get people to understand clues as to what they're about, but more than likely this only helps to explain a very small portion of who we really are. What happens is that when you've labeled yourself modern for instance, it's very hard to get yourselves out of thinking that is who you are. For example, when you go shopping and you see something that's beautiful but let's say from the Victorian era, you may stop yourself from purchasing it. Your instinct told you that you liked it, but your label told you not to buy it. Now granted, the designer in me may have told you that if it was ugly to leave it where you found it, but that's another story all together. The point is that people will always try to place you in a box, don't help them along by handing them the label maker.

The moment you start releasing limitations and boundaries, is the moment you will start seeing your life for what it really is. This is clearer to me now than ever before. It used to come in small glimpses here and there, but it was elusive and I couldn't get a hold of it. But like anything in life, the more you practice and the more intention that you put into something, the more it becomes attainable. Now the glimpses have become my reality and the rest fades into the illusion it always was. That is why the words that I write here are coming from the very core of my being. They are my truth behind the curtain and hopefully they will resonate with you.

Can your dreams become a reality?

Now I'm not telling you to go to the other extreme and turn your house into a fun house full of design mishaps. What I'm saying is that you have to figure out where you stand in your design before you can even start putting the design together. After you have written down all of your thoughts that we have discussed in this chapter, you'll need to translate what they mean into realistic terms. For instance, let's take the earlier example of butterflies. Your dream of butterflies reminded you of how carefree you were as a child and how the warmth of the sun felt so good. You may want to delve into ways that your home could feel happy and warm, possibly through the use of paint colors or fabrics. Maybe introducing flower prints or even real flowers would be a great way to translate this feeling into your home. If you tend to not get a lot of light coming in then maybe you may want to think about changing out your window treatments to ones that allow more light to filter in during the day.

Another thought may be to introduce more nature throughout the home and to try to figure out how to connect the indoors to your outdoors. This comes up a lot in my design work because people are feeling more of a need to connect to their outdoor space. Why...because it makes them happy. A few simple ways I already mentioned, but you can also add things like skylights, even a living plant wall. If you get stumped coming up with ways to translate your ideas, then google some key words on the internet and I'm sure that you'll get a ton of new ideas. One of my favorite websites to use for this is Pinterest. They have great images and their search engine is super easy!

And to think that all of these great ideas started with a simple butterfly! You may go down a bunch of these verbal idea roads, but I ask that when you're done jotting them down, that you circle the ideas that you really love, and that make sense for your space as well as your budget. You'll be surprised at how much you have to work with and how many of them are a really good match for your personality. And since you gave yourself the space to dream first before adding the realistic framework to the equation, then you will be in a much better position to create a space that feels authentic to who you are.

CHAPTER 7
Live like you mean it

Will you live life on purpose, find purpose in your life, or both?

There is no way I could write this book without writing about the reason that motivates me to be who I am. I also understand that this may be the chapter when some of you may toss my book out the window. Ok maybe out the window is a bit much, but at least tossed onto the giveaway pile. But like it or not here we go, so just hear me out. I already spoke to you about my younger years, and how I always knew I wanted to accomplish bigger things in my life. And as great as that dream was to motivating my life onto a positive track, it was nothing compared to the realization that I had, that what I wanted to be in life would be meaningless if I didn't align it with a higher purpose. I'm not talking about religion or about a life without material possessions. Although if that's your calling than I'm not knocking it. I myself like air conditioning and shiny things too much to go down that road. What I'm talking about is creating something positive alongside the creation of your plan.

Both must happen simultaneously for the magic to work. Yes, there are very successful people out there who could care less about giving back in some way. And most of them don't care about leaving something better off than when they started. But those aren't the people I'm talking about. I'm talking about the Oprah's and Mark Zuckerberg's of the world. I'm talking about you and me. There's a saying that's been around forever by Mahatma Gandhi, and it's always resonated in me. The saying goes "Be the change that you wish to see in the world." Now I know you're thinking to yourself that you're not about to run off and start a hunger strike to protest oppression, and guess what, neither am I. But that doesn't mean that you can't do what you love and do some good along the way.

Have you ever had a defining moment?

For me it started with something as simple as wanting to earn enough money to help support my mom. She had sacrificed so much for me and has worked hard her whole life. I imagined myself one day being like those famous rappers that ripped off their parent's blind fold and grandly presented them with a new car or even a new house, with a ginormous big red bow wrapped around it! Ok I know, my imagination is kinda over the top, but I guess that's why they thought I'd make for good TV. Then I read a book that would change my life forever, it was Eckhart Tolle's, *A New Earth*. Actually, the first time I had tried to read it I didn't get it, and I put it down after a few paragraphs. But about a year later I was having a particularly bad day and

I went to one of the only places that makes me feel better, the book store. You thought I was kidding about loving books didn't you. At the time, I lived near this giant Barnes and Nobles, and I would walk in the door and take a deep breath. I would breathe in all of the potential knowledge that was right at my fingertips. It was always exciting to me that I could open a book and escape into another world, or that I could learn something new that I never knew of only hours before. I know I sound like a big dork, but to this day there is nothing that makes me feel the same way.

Anyway, on that day I did what I normally do when I enter a bookstore, I let my instincts take me where I needed to go. It's a little game that I've always played with myself, can't help it. I will just walk around and look at the book spines without reading a word and trail my finger from book to book, until I feel a jolt of energy or even a tingling sensation in my fingers. And when I do, I pull out the book I have my hand on. In order for the game to work you can't read the book titles, no cheating allowed. You can only register colors and feeling. Ok so some of you may think I'm nuts but I like to use my other senses and not just the literal ones. I find that your intuition knows more than your brain and if you just open yourself up to listening to it, then you can discover a whole world that you never knew existed. You actually do it all the time and you don't even realize it. Every time your phone rings, before you look at it to see who's calling, a name may pop up in your head. I'm not saying you're always right, I'm just saying that it's the same intuition muscle that you're flexing.

On this day, I pulled out Eckhart Tolle's, *A New Earth* and I opened the book and read the first line that jumped out at me.

Now don't quote me, but it basically said that the information in this book will only be understood when you are ready to accept it. That's seriously what it said, and you know what, I listened. I sat my butt down on the floor on the same spot that I was just standing on, and I began to read. I couldn't put it down, and what I found boring a year earlier, I found mind-blowing that day. He spoke about awakening to our life's purpose and about how abundance without a greater purpose will always leave us empty. When I was done reading his book I knew that I would never look at my life the same. How could I? There are these moments in life that you know will define you. It doesn't have to be a big moment, but you came to the other side of it changed. I always think it's funny how you could feel like the world stopped but you were the only one who saw it. I looked around and wanted to shout out everything that I was now aware of. But somehow everyone was still walking around and going about their day. The only other time that this feeling occurs is when someone dies. Anyone who has lost a loved one knows what I'm talking about. Like somehow the world should have stopped when they did, but somehow it didn't.

Sorry to take a sad side road there but the feeling needed to be acknowledged. Let's get back to my discovery. I realized two very important things while reading that book, one was that I still wanted my big dreams, and two was that I wanted, no, needed, to give something back. We all have different ways that this could manifest for us. And just like no two people are the same, how you apply your imprint on this world is unique. All of these ideas started making houses in my head. I wanted to give young girls the help that I never had in my industry. I wanted to be the best version of Blanche that I could be, but to also show people all of the battle scars it takes to truly find success in being who you are. I promised myself that I would help others along the way to my dreams, and once I reached my dreams, I was going to give back. I realized that by creating and living in a positive space and by living my dreams, that I was inspiring others to do the same. This was my path and my true purpose. Yes, I still wanted to be uber-successful and have nice things...and maybe a compound full of rescue animals. But with the clarity came the knowledge that none of that would matter if I didn't create a life with a positive purpose.

How many mood bombs do you drop?

Like I mentioned before, this could manifest in a different way for you. It could start out as simple as being less grouchy in the morning when you walk into work. I know this sounds trivial, but how you greet the world sends off a chain reaction. It's like when you're in a great mood and you run into someone who's in a crappy mood. You exchange a few "hellos" and "how's your day going," and next thing you know you're walking away in a crappy mood. *Boom*, you've been hit with a kamikaze mood bomb! But it doesn't end there, the rest of the day you're dropping mood bombs everywhere you go. See how something so simple can snowball and affect so many people. I always say, keep your energy in check! I use this simple example because there are many of you out there who are probably reading this book and thinking that you work at the same job and live in the same house that you've always have and you don't see it changing anytime soon. But all it takes are little adjustments to feel more fulfilled. It can be anything from how you approach your day, how you treat people, recycling, or passing on some of your hard-earned knowledge.

The difference you will soon find is that instead of simply existing, you will thrive. If you are reading the words that I am writing, then you, like me, do not simply want to exist in the "good." The person who is "good" is the same person who is just glad they are not sick, but they're not great either. You ask them how they are, and their response is "I'm good". Boo I say! I want to thrive, don't you?

Are your patterns on repeat?

I was talking to a friend the other night and we were in one of our more philosophical conversations. I'm not going to lie, sometimes our conversations run more along the lines of which Real Housewives episode we caught the night before. But this conversation was about changing the patterns in your life and where to even start. I said something that ten years ago would have been a foreign concept to me, but that today was a daily practice. I said "it all starts with becoming the watcher of yourself, and once you do, you can start to release patterns that no longer serve you." I think we were both surprised at that pearl of wisdom that popped out of my mouth. I must have eaten my spinach that day.

I've been thinking about what I said ever since. Not because of the message but because of how the message has shaped me throughout the years. When I first read about this concept, and yes, it's been around for centuries, I didn't make it up; I'm just smart enough to apply it. Anyway, when I first read about this concept, that's all it felt like to me, a concept. I thought "How do I become the watcher?" I had lots of patterns in my life that I felt were blocking my success and the life that I truly wanted. I felt like there was this magical land that I knew others had found, but I couldn't even find the keys to get out of my house.

I knew enough to know what I didn't want, but how did I stop repeating the patterns that led me back to zero? I realized that I could have all of the information at my disposal but I would always choose the wrong door if I didn't change the "why" in my decisions. To change your patterns, you have to first learn what they are, and to do that you have to be present. I don't mean in attendance physically, I mean in attendance mentally and emotionally. You know what I'm talking about because we all do it. You're in a familiar situation; it's actually a reoccurring situation that always leaves you wondering why does this keep happening to me? And when the spotlights is on you (figuratively of course) your brain goes on auto pilot. Why? Because autopilot is comfortable and why make things difficult and do something different and scary.

You may think that I'm going to suggest something crazy like make different decisions. That would be insane! Well I'm not... yet. What I'm asking is that you take a moment in the midst of this event, or if that's too much then after it's occurred, to step outside of the situation and look at yourself like you would a stranger. The reason I called this an event is because it is. It's the smaller moments and decisions that shape our lives more than the bigger ones ever will. It's the decisions you make when you feel like no one is watching you. It's the moment that won't ruin your life, it will just change the course of it.

Take note of these moments; notice the common thread that they all carry. All it takes are small adjustments to create change.

If you try to reach for grand gestures, they may not take, but slight shifts are more manageable. Notice your energy and what feelings you had during these moments; they are the indicators to your motives for why you chose one path over the other. You have to get to the root of the decision in order to make a shift. I promise you that it gets easier. Something just clicks like it did for me and you get a glimpse of clarity that leaves you thinking "I don't need to do this anymore." I always refer to the quote that states that the definition of insanity is doing the same thing over and over again and expecting a different outcome. Think about it, because that quote has given me the kick in the butt that I have sometimes needed throughout my life. Your life doesn't just happen to you, you consciously choose your life with every decision you make. If you don't believe me, then next time something happens in your life that leaves you wondering why God hates you, think about the actions that led up to that result. I'm not talking about things like death and taxes, so stop making that face.

Can an old dog learn new tricks?

They say that when you are starting a new workout routine to get into shape that it takes about six weeks for your body to start to build up a memory. After the first six weeks then your body craves the endorphins that are released from the actual workout. It's no different from when you are training your brain to learn a new pattern. I'm not going to lie to you, it's not easy. Our brain is constantly pushing back on every positive thought we have with a "poo-poo" negative thought. But every time that happens, you have to than one up it and reinforce the positive thought again. I talk to people all the time who tell me stories of how they read books like

"The Secret" and said their daily mantra's but nothing ever changed. It's not that they didn't believe in what they were saying; it's that they didn't believe it was true for them.

You see, you have to start somewhere, and that somewhere is writing down the dreams and goals, saying the words out loud, reading the books for encouragement, and visualizing the life you know is just on the other side of the curtain. But then comes the hard part; which is believing that all of these things can be true for you. The next exercise is simple but must be done on a regular basis.

Exercise 7: Every time you have a limiting or negative thought about yourself or your potential, I want you to replace it or turn it around to a positive thought. At first you may have to repeat it to yourself a few times, because you're programmed to believe the negative. There are two very specific times that this will constantly come up for you; it will always come up when you are planning for or visualizing the life you're going after, and it will come up when you are in the action of making a goal a reality.

I'll give you a personal example of using this method that again I did not invent but will gladly apply since it works like a charm once you give it a chance. Years ago I was working out of my tiny one-bedroom apartment and came to the realization that I needed more space for my growing business. I would daydream about the perfect home office situation, how I would feel, and especially how I would decorate it. But with that realization also came the reality that more space meant more money. I mean I was picking up traction and work was going well…but what if it all stopped and I couldn't make rent...and then I'd be living on the street in a cardboard box with two cats and a Chihuahua. Ok I got a little dramatic there again, but really, it's where my mind goes. I wanted the space more than I was scared, so every time I would just replace the thought with the visualization of having everything I needed. I would even say to myself out loud "I have everything that I need to support my dreams." So, when I actually came across the perfect place by chance one day and had to sign the lease, guess what popped into my head? The "you're never going to be able to afford this place" voice, along with the images of my chihuahua with his tin cup outside on the sidewalk. I just pulled my internal voice back to my "I have everything that I need to support my dreams" follow up. Just like that *Bam!* I kicked the other voice's butt.

We are all human and so you're always going to have your fears and insecurities. Sometime your fears are there for a good reason but you can override the thought and replace them with ones that will motivate you and not tear you down. When you are trying to change behavior, you can't take something away without replacing it. It's how they teach people to overcome addiction (which by the way this is). The only way to effectively take away something negative is to replace it with something positive.

If you don't believe in it and in you, how can you expect someone else to? You need to sell yourself first before you can sell anybody else on the idea. This especially goes for convincing the universe that it needs to work in conjunction with you to give you everything that you need or for that matter, want.

CHAPTER 8

Ebbs and flows

Living through the answers is a lot like waiting for paint to dry.

hate not being busy and I especially hate not being busy and being broke. It feels like you can run around chasing leads and making moves all day long but nothing...and I mean nothing. . .is working out. Trying to stay positive when your life is in the middle of an "Ebb" is as easy as (as my father used to say) pissing in the wind. When you're on your game everything works out, it's like you can't do anything wrong. I love the hustle of it all, it's the energy of movement that really excites me and pushes me to go bigger and be better. But we all know that what goes up must come down. It doesn't always stay down but it does feel like it always will.

Are you prepared to succeed?

I used to believe, and I'm pretty sure we all have, that when nothing is going good in our lives, that nothing will ever be good again. We all know that those feelings are based out of fear and not in reality. Since I'm kinda a Type A (if you haven't already figured it out), I learned a long time ago that these "Ebbs" are a blessing in disguise. When you're running around taking over the world you never have time to pause and prepare for your next move, or pause so you can sharpen your skills or even reorganize to work smarter. Well this is when you are handed that "time" on a silver platter. It just may not feel like a gift at the time. You just have to flip your thinking from the "this sucks" mode to the "get ready" mode. There's another saying (can you tell I love sayings) that says there is no such thing as luck, just the moment when preparation meets opportunity. These are the situations that they are talking about.

The alternative is sitting and brooding about how no one is calling and nothing is happening. Ok so since that idea stinks, let's try to keep your mind off it, and get your life and maybe even your house in order so that when the next wave comes, you're in prime position to ride it. If you're like me and are self-employed, not being busy can mean lots and lots of free time. So, I just treat my down time like I would as if I was busy. I make a list (yes, another list) of all the things that I could benefit from doing now that I have the time. My list may include ways to bring in more business, or maximize on the current business that I have. You have a better chance of upselling to the clients whom already know and trust you than you are to strangers. I always look into continuing education seminars that will teach me something new that could benefit my clients. And you don't have to limit yourself to work-related education; you may have always wanted to learn a second language or to take pottery or cooking classes.

I always like to de-clutter and reorganize my space. I mean just because it's been working doesn't mean you can't find ways to improve it. A big one for me is volunteering at a local non-profit. There are plenty of ways to give back and they are right in your own back yard. There are also lots of local meet-up and social groups that are great for networking. I just saw one in my area for a group of local organic produce growers. There is literally something for everyone, and you never know who you're going to meet. I've had all sorts of opportunities come from putting myself out there and attending social groups. I've met new clients, created partnerships, and made new friends. I try to keep motivated by doing one thing a day that gives me the feeling of accomplishment. It can be a small thing like an email or reading something that I didn't know the day before. The little wins are just as important as the big ones. In fact, they are more important because the little ones are the fuel to get you to the big ones. Don't think it has to be these huge moves that make the day a success. I've lived off of a "happiness high" for days from something as simple as looking into a new workshop.

I like to use this time to fill in the gaps that can't be filled when I'm in overload "hustle" mode. My last "Ebb" gave me time to think about the next direction I wanted to take. I was also able to see how I was overlooking ways to increase my company cash flow. I would have never had thought of these ideas if my life didn't give me the space that I may not have wanted, but definitely needed in order to do so. I can't write this chapter without telling you a funny story that just shows how we all think.

My mom works with me and so she is not only witness to my wins but she also has a front row seat to my fails. This is especially true when we as a company are not busy. To say that I am my mother's daughter is taking it lightly. She is the true master of multitasking and making busy look like you're at the beach. I've always admired her skills, and without even realizing it I have become my mother...we all do. Thank goodness I have a savvy yet sometimes intimidating mom, and I inherited that too...just ask my contractors. Anyway, recently we were super slow, so slow you could hear tumble weeds rolling past our desks. She literally turned to me and asked "what if we never get another client?" As if I wasn't stressed enough and maybe a small part of me will always have that fear, every entrepreneur does.

In fact, we all have the fear that it's never going to turn around and get better. But if you're reading this book then that means you're never going to let that happen. You're going to make the time work in your favor, because you believe in what you are doing and in what you want. So sometimes that takes patience and fortitude, and the need to understand that instead of fighting the current, the best thing that you can do is surrender to the flow that you are being pulled along in at the moment. Nothing last forever and once you understand that even in the best of times when you are riding high that that too won't last forever, then you can find your balance. Understand that there will be ups and downs, but be wise enough to take advantage when you're up and strong enough to hold on when you're down, because both do not last very long.

It's that kind of self-awareness that will be your rock when it feels like you're standing all alone. That's what it can feel like, that you're all alone in trying to keep your head up. All you have to do to show yourself that you will get through to the other side is to look behind you. If you looked back to all of the highs and lows in your life you will have proof that you have what it takes to make it through, because you're here right now and your fine. At this moment, nothing is physically wrong and you're not in any danger. The only thing that can get to you if you allow it to is the fear, the fear of the future and of what may or may not happen to you. If you can allow yourself to be in the moment and understand that you are all good, and that you can handle whatever is thrown your way, then you will find some peace within the temporary chaos in your mind.

The very first book on self-awareness taught me this. Again, it was Eckhart Tolle and it was his book called *The Power of Now*. If you find yourself at the moment in one of life's "Ebbs" then I strongly suggest picking up a copy. It will help you to put your current circumstance into perspective. Every time I find myself starting to feel a sense of panic about life in general, I always go back to what I was taught. These are all tools we pick up along the way to pull out of our tool box when we need them in different life situations. Hopefully this book gives you a cliff notes version of my favorite tools that I have picked up along the way to support me in becoming a successful person who is happy with the life that I am currently creating. Work in progress people!

Don't lose your balance

Everything that you are reading in this book will be impossible to do, if you don't give yourself the support that you need to be at your best. This includes showing yourself compassion, getting the rest that you need, making healthy and positive decisions, and knowing when to say no. How can you ask anyone else, including the universe to support you, if you aren't walking the walk? A person treats their body how they treat their life. Unhealthy body equals an unhealthy life. How can you have the will to make sacrifices and make decisions that honor your best self when you can't even respect your body and mind? We are complex beings and we need certain types of fuel in order to work at our optimal speed. It's a lifestyle and I'm here to give you the tools to create a balance that works for you. There's not a one plan fits all type of thing going on here. It's about compromising, and listening to what your body needs. Here is where we get in tune with what we need, when we need it.

I am one cranky lady when I don't treat myself right. Lack of sleep, no workouts, and running on the hamster wheel without a break makes the pop rocks break out of the box I call my head. I know I'm not the only one who feels this way, but I've noticed that most people ignore the signs until it's too late. Well just like there are the ebb's and flows of life, the same is true for your body and brain. I am going to blow your mind right now with a revelation. I am a very introverted person…who also happens to be an extroverted person…when I want to be. I love nothing more than locking myself in my house with my Chihuahua (aka: the bite-size furry love of my life) with hours of The Real Housewives of "all and any state" on my DVR, and ignore everyone. Even text messages annoy me at these moments. This may be because I have a career that requires me to be "On" most of the time. I am the go-to person for my clients, my staff, and even some of my friends. You know who you are, but in your defense, I do like to talk a lot, so I would blab to me too! I need to honor both parts of me to be balanced and happy. If I'm having an intense week, then I need at least one afternoon or evening to myself. Even a few minutes will help keep everything running smoothly and keep me from losing it!

Healthy eating and breaking a sweat is also super important. "But I don't wanna get off the sofa and put the Cheetos down!" you may say…But I promise you that if you just try eating a bit better and working it out, that you will start to feel more energized and… well… just great! I don't know all of the technical terms but basically your endorphins kick in and you start to feel like a rock star, and since you'll be looking all sexy, you'll feel like a hot mama-jama in no time! That's as much of a technical explanation as I'm going to give you. To me it's about feeling great. If you feel great then you'll be in a better mood, and you'll end up making better choices. Don't be too strict with yourself, I mean don't slam down a Big Mac every night and call it a cheat snack either. But find a rhythm that feels right. You'll know when you've fallen into your groove. You'll feel rested and the stresses of your day will feel manageable.

I'm a big believer in saying no to things and saying yes to me when I need it. It's hard the first time you try it but it gets easier. Everyone gets so used to running on empty that they forget to fill up the tank. You're never going to get anywhere on empty. Treat yourself once in a while to a massage or a facial. I'm even talking to the guys out there. Yes manly men can get facials; it's not just for chicks. You can thank me later when you realize that life is meaningless without it. I actually truly believe that. Take a few moments, heck, take a whole day for yourself. Not a day to run errands or work on your to-do list. I mean take a day to re-connect. Just between you and me, as I write this, today was a work day, and I just hung out with Maddox (my chihuahua for those who just tuned in) and chilled out. It was fantastic and exactly what I needed after a crazy week. I was in such a good mood that it motivated me to get to work on this chapter, which by chance had me blocked for a good while.

When you take care of the small things before they turn into big things, then that's when true balance is achieved. You can goal set until you're blue in the face and climb all of the mountains in your way, but without knowing how to ride the everyday waves of ups and downs and keeping your balance, then the sea of life will swallow you under before you even peak. Every morning check in with yourself and ask yourself "What do I need today?" "How do I feel?" "What small step can I do to keep my motivation alive?" The answers may surprise you.

CHAPTER 9

Life's punch list

Thoughts without actions are called dreams.
(FYI: I didn't come up with that but I wish I did)

et's go through a summary of what we spoke about. It seems like a lot to take in but let's break it down into manageable steps. On my projects I usually have a walkthrough with my design clients, where we make a punch list of everything that's left to do, and we review what we already have plans to do; we will create the same for your life. People always ask me how I get so much done and how do I remember everything. It's so simple that everyone can do it, and the truly successful people do it every day. We make lists—it sounds basic—but it's impossible to remember everything. I'm a very visual person and so when I want to make sure I get something done, I make a list. I even go one step further like tacking my list on my wall or by my computer. If you came to my office right now you would see at the top of my priority list, the words "write book." And if you look at my phone calendar you would see a time blocked out for "write at least one chapter of book." So, grab your pen and pad and let's button this up!

Before we get to mapping out your day-to-day, you first and foremost have to tackle exercises one through seven. So here they are again, because (a) repetition helps things to stick; and (b) I just dropped a lot of knowledge on you and you may need a quick recap.

Exercise 1: Who Are You?
Exercise 2: What Do You Want?
Exercise 3: What's The Worst Case Scenario?
Exercise 4: Making Big Plans
Exercise 5: The Post-It Note Challenge
Exercise 6: Do YOU Live Here?
Exercise 7: Flip The Script

Going through all of those exercises will really help you to zone in on what you want and better yet, why you want the things that you do. If we just leave these thoughts in our head, they can get all jumbled up and messy. But when you put them on paper, then you make some sense out of them. It's less confusing and really can bring things into focus.

You got a pretty good idea of how to plan for a goal in Exercise 4: Making Big Plans. I want you to take that outline and apply it to your top listed goal items that you really want to achieve first. You may be thinking "But Blanche there are too many!" Break it down into manageable steps. Let's say you have ten to twenty goals that you would love to accomplish in life. Just start out with the top three. You can always weave another one into the mix if one of your top three gets stagnant, and vice versa, you can always take one off the list. This is your life we are talking about, so things will shift, and you can change your mind at any time. That's the beauty of it; you can go at your own pace. Making a list is just a daily reminder that your goals and dreams are real and that you are accomplishing real tasks to manifest them!

Remember for each goal you write at the top of the page, you will write smaller everyday tasks that can help you get to the big goal. You will make this type of list for every goal. This is a working list and so there will be a lot of crossing out and re-writes. Unless you write them digitally, then there will just be a lot of deletes. But I can't stress enough that I recommend you actually using a pen and paper. I know it may sound Stone Age to some of you but this list has to be in your face every day. If you keep it on your phone, IPad or computer, then you can close it and not look at it for days. I want this list taped on your wall, by your desk, by your bed, or even in your kitchen. Wherever you're going to see it every day no matter what. The list will keep you honest, trust me.

There are days that life is so busy that it gets in the way. But there staring at me is my list! I swear it stares at me, and I can hear it saying "Blanche what about me? Did you forget that you have dreams that aren't getting any younger?" Ok maybe my imagination goes all GI-Jane on me, but at least it's effective. Also, nothing feels better than crossing something off your list. That's why it's important to write small tasks that you can do every day. Crossing them off will give you a sense of satisfaction and just plain happy motivation. Because it may take a while to reach the big goal and if you don't feel like you've accomplished anything along the way, you can lose motivation. You see there is no quick fix to making your dreams happen. You have to have patience, but you also need to feel motivated along the way. It's not just the end goal that is worth it, but the journey has to feel worth it too. In between all of these goals is something called your life. And if you're not enjoying the journey, then you may discover that you may not enjoy the destination as much as you thought either. The smaller wins that you can tackle every day will help you feel inspired.

Here's an example of what one goal should look like, and some of the topics and questions that you should be covering on your way to accomplishing your goal.

Goal: Start Own Business

TASK: Find a Mentor

- Research successful people that I can benefit from
- Email and make appointments to create a connection
- Schedule regular appointments to brainstorm
- Look into more than one mentor (Think Tank?)

TASK: Investigate Comparable Business Models

- Join networking groups in my industry
- Visit local businesses in my field
- Do online research for public data on my field

TASK: Create Business Plan

- Create a timeline
- Figure out how much I will need to get my business off the ground
- Do I need an investor?
- Where is my start up capitol coming from (Bank or Other)?
- Figure out who is my client
- How will I market?
- How much do I need to bring in to keep my business running?
- Will I need to hire or do I outsource?
- What tasks can I accomplish on my own to keep costs down?

TASK: Create a Branding Package

- What is my business model?
- What will my brand be known for and how will people see us?
- What is my marketing strategy?
- How much money do I need to create my marketing package?
- Create Marketing Material: business card, website, logo
- Find vendors to create my marketing material

TASK: Location

- Will I be web based or brick and mortar?
- Find location options
- Figure out how much space I will need
- Connect with a Realtor and a Bank
- Look into comparable businesses around the chosen location

You get the picture. I write down all of the things, even the mental tasks and questions, that I need to think about to achieve the big stuff. I treat everything as a task, everything is written down. This way you have turned mental chaos into manageable steps. It's clear on paper, and it's all of the steps you have to take. I am constantly adding and taking away from my lists. It keeps it fresh and manageable. Don't be discouraged if some tasks take longer than others. The lists are there to help guide you in a direction but life sometimes has other plans. So be loose with how you get to your goals, follow your instincts, pat yourself on the back, and try not to judge yourself too much. At the end of the day we want dreams because we feel that they will fulfill us and make us happy. But the secret is that you have to figure out a way to find happiness and fulfillment in the everyday. The big dreams are much more amazing when they are just the cherry on top!

Jump off The Cliff

This is the part where you mentally jump off the cliff (please don't try to jump off a real cliff!). If you devote 15 minutes a day to the plans that we worked on in this book, then you will get further than you did yesterday. It's easy to get discouraged once you take the leap and start the steps, because you think nothing's happening. But I am a big believer in the fact that once you make a conscious decision to move in a direction, the universe will conspire to help you make it happen. You didn't get the life you are living now over-night, so you have to work a little bit each day to get to the life that you deserve. The energy alone that you will put into the universe will set things in motion, but your actions will support that energy, and before you know it your life will never be the same. Now go kick some booty and make your dreams happen!

If you enjoyed this book, leave me a review and be sure to tell everyone that you have ever met about it! Word of mouth is an indie author's best friend.

www.bgarciadesigns.com
Facebook
Instagram
Twitter

Mom & Dad in the 70's. Those sideburns!

Me on a volunteer building project. The jeans and glasses say it all!

I was such a ham. My banana was my microphone.

Dad as a kid in New York

Printed in Great Britain
by Amazon